BESTSELLING WRITER AND EDITOR SUSAN POLIS SCHUTZ SELECTS THE VERY BEST WRITINGS TO TOUCH YOU, MOVE YOU, CHANGE YOU...FOREVER

"In high emotion...the reigning star is Susan Polis Schutz."
—*TIME*

"Heartfelt...just about says it all....Here are voices that sing of growth, of devotion, of motherhood in its finest flower."
—*The Book Page* on *Mother, I Will Always Love You*

"Susan's work continues to touch the hearts of millions across the world, sharing patience and joy, peace and love to people everywhere....In a world filled with uncertainty, war and disease, famine and fear, Susan Polis Schutz is reminding people that a little love can go a long way."
—*True Story*

"A poet of the heart."
—*Family Weekly*

Books By Susan Polis Schutz

To My Son With Love
To My Daughter With Love
I Love You

Also edited by Susan Polis Schutz

Mother, I Will Always Love You
Don't Ever Stop Dreaming Your Dreams
To My Father With Love

Published By

WARNER BOOKS

Mother, I Love You Forever

A Collection of Poems
Edited by Susan Polis Schutz

WARNER BOOKS

A Time Warner Company

Warner Books, Inc., 1271 Avenue of the Americas, New York, NY 10020

🅦 A Time Warner Company

Printed in the United States of America
First Warner Books Printing: May 1994
10 9 8 7 6 5 4 3 2 1

Library of Congress Cataloging-in-Publication Data
Mother, I love you forever / edited by Susan Polis Schutz.
    p. cm.
  ISBN 0-466-67018-9
  1. Mother and Child--Poetry. 2. Mothers--Poetry. 3. American poetry. I. Schutz, Susan Polis.
PS595.M64M65 1993
811.008'0352042--dc20   93-50214
                                                              CIP

CONTENTS

I Love You Forever, Mother

You have shown me how to give of myself
You have shown me leadership
You have taught me to be strong
You have taught me the importance of the family
You have demonstrated unconditional love
You have demonstrated a sensitivity
    to people's needs
You have handed down to me the important
    values in life
You have handed down to me the idea
    of achieving one's goals
You have set an example, throughout your life
of what a mother and woman should be like
    I am so proud of you
        and I love you
            forever

— Susan Polis Schutz

Thank You for
All Your Love and for
All You've Done for Me

Words can hardly express
all that you mean to me
and all you've done for me
   through these years.
I've realized, as I get older,
that you're not only my mother,
   but you are my friend also,
and that is very precious to me.
Not everyone has a friendship
   with their mother.
I know that I always have you
to talk over any problem I have
and that you will listen
and give me the best advice you have,
   what you think is best for me.

We both get moody and have
    our bad days,
but our love still stays strong,
and we understand each other better
    every day.
Thank you for all that you are,
for being the best mother
    you know how to be,
for always listening,
for all your love and affection,
and for all you've done for me.

—Chris Eichenauer

To My Mother — I Love You

You come to mind so often . . .
and I wonder why I have been chosen
to have a wonderful, loving
    parent like you.

You have given me love . . .
    welcoming me home with open arms.
You have given me courage . . .
    helping me in times of need.
You have given me security . . .
    knowing I have a safe home and
    a special family to return to always.
You have given me trust . . .
    from always being able to
    believe in me, and I in you.
You have given me honesty . . .
    knowing that we always speak
    the truth with each other.
And you have given me friendship . . .
    helping me to realize that I am
        never alone; you are always near.
I want so much to repay you
for your kindness,
and someday I will find a way . . .
but for now I can only tell you,
    though I don't always show it
        and though I don't always say it . . .
            I love you.

— Lisa Ford

In Your Footsteps, Mother

Mother, my words of love to you are
not just for any special occasion, but
because there is a very special bond
between mother and child.
I remember so long ago when I
followed so closely behind you . . .
you protected my every move
while holding my hand, and
your love never failed me.
As I've grown from year to year,
your hand opened to allow my
reaching out and growth.
You watched me strive and achieve,
with so much pride and silent prayer.
You also let me fail on my own,
but were always there to pick me up
while we shared the tears.

Maybe words can never fulfill
just how much is in my heart, but
I want you to know that I've learned
so much from you, and silently

I will always reflect, with smiles
    and grateful tears,
upon our moments together.
I've realized that I may no longer
follow behind you as I did when I
was small; instead, our footsteps
have become equal strides as we
walk side by side, together in friendship.
Mother, I don't know if I can ever
repay you for the gifts of life.
But if I can live my life by giving
to others as much as you have
    given to me . . .
I will be following in your footsteps
    once again.

— Danine Winkler

Dear Mother,
I know it's not your birthday
or your anniversary
or even Mother's Day.
It's just an ordinary day.
I don't need any money,
and I don't have a problem
to solve . . .
I just wanted
to say,
"I love you."

— Deanna Beisser

Whenever I'm
Away from Home, Mother

Your love for your mother
is something that you
never completely comprehend
until you are
    separated by the miles
from her warmth
    and her wonder.

When I was living at home,
I took so many things
    for granted
    without ever meaning to.
And I always knew
what a precious person you were,
but I never really took the time
to go beyond the thought . . .
    and into what you really
        meant to me.

Now that I'm without you
by my side, I find myself
thinking of you so often . . .
hoping in a way that it will
bring you a little closer to me.

And in those thoughts
I always come to the conclusion
that you are more than my mother;
you're a counselor and a companion;
you're a dear friend and a happy home;
you're a thousand beautiful memories;
    and you're someone whom I love
        with all my heart.

— Collin McCarty

Mother,
as you well know,
I have become involved
   in too many things,
and I don't write to you
as often as I should.
Maybe you wonder, at times,
if I have forgotten you
and if I need you less than I used to,
and I can understand
how I might cause you to feel that way.
It's true that I am very busy
much of the time,
but I never get too busy to tell
my friends what a wonderful mother
I have,
and that without you,
I would have nothing,
because you are everything to me.
   And no matter how full my life gets,
      it could never be as full
         as my heart is —
            with love for you.

— Ann Rudacille

Mother . . . I've always
   wanted you to know
my special feelings for you.

Growing up was hard for me.
I know I was a difficult child,
but what got me through
   and what made me okay
was knowing you were
   always there.

I'll never forget
   the caring in your eyes.
You let me grow and
   allowed me to explore.
I love you for
   letting me be me.

Your life touches mine
            every day . . .
in the way I look,
    the words I speak . . .
they have all come from you
        in some special way.

I am so
    thankful for you, Mother.

You are the gift
    that I was born with.

— Shirley Paceley

For You, Mother

I want to thank you, Mother,
because a long time ago, you gave me
the most precious gift I'll ever
    receive — my life.
It's a gift I can share with others,
a gift that grows in value over time.
Thank you for enabling me to receive
    all the love showered upon me,
not only today, but every day;
for enabling me to experience all
    that life has to offer . . .
your love, my time, life's beauty.
You have given me the most promising,
    useful gift,
the gift I celebrate today and every day.
    Mother . . .
        thank you for me.

— Barbara Lemke

For Mother, with all my heart

I have always kept
my feelings for you
   in the most precious place
             within me.

There is a place in my heart
that learned,
   from the very beginning,
          what love was all about.
Whether you know it or not,
   you taught me a beautiful lesson about life:
      that giving is receiving, and that the circle
      of love is never as complete
      as it is in a family like ours.

My memories of home
   go with me wherever I go,
      and they keep me close to you . . .

   I know that I
      will never stop thanking you
         for everything you are to me
            and for everything you do.

— Collin McCarty

Here Are Seven Reasons Why
It's Great to Be Your Child

—You are the best mother
anyone could ever hope to have.
—Your wonderful qualities have made
a lasting impression on me that I
will admire for as long as I live.
—You give me so much to be thankful for.
—You have wisdom that goes beyond
your words, a sweetness that goes
beyond your smile, and a heart
of pure gold.
—You take the time to hear my deepest
thoughts, my feelings, and my fears.
—You've dried tears no one else could see,
you've helped me find happiness,
and you've taught me that I really can
make some of my dreams come true.
—There isn't a child in all
the world who could ask for
a more beautiful mother . . . than you.

—Chris Gallatin

In Appreciation
for Everything You Do, Mother

I came into this world and you were there
to love and protect me;
I came into this world and you were there
to make my way safe and secure.
You were there to encourage and reward me
for my accomplishments.
You gave of yourself
through times of limited finances,
through times when you were tired or ill,
through times when you sacrificed for me.
You established strong goals,
living as an example of
what you expected of your children.

You were my greatest teacher,
shaping my strengths and weaknesses
into the feelings and values I have today.

If I am kind,
it is because you taught me.
If I have patience,
it is because you exhibited it.
If I have wisdom,
it is because you believed in me.
I came into this world and you were there,
and I am better for it.

—Edith Bodkin Frederick

To My Mother

For as long as I can remember
you were always by my side
to give me support
to give me confidence
to give me help

For as long as I can remember
you were always the person
    I looked up to
so strong
so sensitive
so pretty

For as long as I can remember
and still today
you are everything
a mother should be

For as long as I can remember
you always provided stability
    within our family
full of laughter
full of tears
full of love

So much of what I have become
is because of you
and I want you to know
that I appreciate you, thank you
and love you
more than words can express

— Susan Polis Schutz

A Mother's Love
Is Never-Ending

A mother's love cannot be compared,
for hers is an ever-constant love,
unlimited, unchanging,
and forever.
A mother will hold you while you cry,
soothe you with kind words
when it seems the rest of the world
has turned against you.
A mother will love you when you think
it's impossible that anyone could;
no matter what you have done or said
or failed to do or say,
a mother truly forgives.
A mother will lift your spirits
when you feel there is no hope,
give you confidence and strength
to begin again, and make you laugh
when you think you'll never smile again.
A mother will stand by your side
even when she stands alone;
she will take you as you are,
and never ask for more
than your love in return.

—Flo Fessler

If I could give you the world, I would.
If there were a gift to say
"thank you" for how well you raised me,
I would send it.
But I don't think there could ever be
anything I could give or say
to equal the love and gratitude
I feel for you.
I hope that our relationship shows
how much I treasure you,
and how much your words of wisdom
and support mean to me.

Every day, I thank God for you.
I love your smile, and your hug
that makes everything seem better.
I love the way you've touched my life,
how you've always been a part of it.
I love you,
and I carry your love in my heart every day
for strength and guidance and courage.
It fills me with pride and joy
to have you as my mother.

—Cindy Cabral

To Mother, with Love

You were always there
whenever I needed you.
Caringly, patiently, and lovingly,
you showed me right from wrong.
You helped me to develop values
that became the solid foundation
upon which I continue to build.

Not only did you offer encouragement,
but you also cheered and praised me
on to success.

Because you made me feel
special and important,
I have been able to regard myself
with respect and know
that I am a worthwhile individual.

Many passing seasons have caused me
to see and understand more clearly,
and to more fully appreciate
the constancy of your guidance.

Thank you, Mother, for giving me
a priceless heirloom — your love.

— Lenore Turkeltaub

Mother

Whenever I have a problem, it
    becomes our problem.
You support me in whatever decisions
    I make,
and even when I'm wrong, you stand
    beside me
because you realize that's when I
    need you the most.
Your belief in me is so strong
that you've made me believe in
    myself.
Even though I am no longer a child,
you are still helping me to grow.
I can always depend on you,
not just because you're my parent,
but because you're also my friend.

— Sheilah D. Street

Mother, you'll always be in my heart . . .

When someone cares about their family
as much as I care about mine,
that caring is the result of so many things . . .
of thousands of precious memories,
of love given from the heart,
of being like best friends to each other.

It's a love that is nurtured from
lives that will always be intertwined . . .
through all joy and every sorrow,
beyond today, in each tomorrow,
always cheering each other on,
always helping and hoping for the best.

I don't know if other people feel
as strongly about their family
as I care about ours — I just remember
loving everything about it
from the very start. And that love
is something I will keep
and cherish forever . . .
in the home that will always be
in my heart.

— Collin McCarty

My Ideal Mother

An ideal mother should be
strong and guiding
understanding and giving
An ideal mother should be
honest and forthright
confident and able
An ideal mother should be
relaxed and soft
flexible and tolerant
But most of all
an ideal mother should be a
loving woman
who is always there when needed
and who
by being happy and satisfied
with herself
is able to be happy and loving
with her children
Mother, you are a rare woman —
you are everything an
ideal mother should be

— Susan Polis Schutz

Sometimes, when children grow up,
the time they can share with their mother
is limited.
And even when they find the time,
they don't seem to find the words.
But today I want to share
these words with you, and
I want you to remember them always . . .

I am proud and thankful
that you are the woman
who raised me.
I'll never forget the love
you have shown me
or your constant support
and encouragement.
You always believe in me,
and that has helped me
to become the person I am.
Our relationship
may seem to have changed
over the years,
but I know our love hasn't.
The bond we share can't be changed;
we are together even when we are apart,
for you are forever in my heart,
and I love you.

—Barbara Cage

This Is Our Prayer
as Mother and Child

These are our wishes, our dreams:
That we may always be more than
    close; that nothing will come
    between the bond of love we share.
That I will always be there for you,
    as you will be for me.
That we will listen with love.
That we will share truths and
    tenderness.
That we will trust, and talk things out.
That we will understand.

That wherever you go, you will be
    in my heart,
and your hand will be
    in my hand.

—Laurel Atherton

For you, Mother

Ever since
I've been old enough
    to remember,
you have been there
whenever I needed you . . .
    to share my troubles
    to laugh with me
        when I was happy
    to love me most
        when I was hurt.
So many memories . . .
memories I hold most dear,
and that will be cherished forever.
For not only have you been
    my mother
    and my best friend,
    but also the woman
    I most want to be like
        in life.

— Debbie Avery

To My Mother

You were always there
to help me
You were always there
to guide me
You were always there
to laugh with me
You were always there
to cry with me
But most important
you were always
there to love me
And believe me
I am always
here to love you

—Susan Polis Schutz

I'm Glad
You're My Mother

I sometimes wonder what kind of person
I'd be, if for some reason you had not
been my mother.
I think of the values I might have been
taught, and I wonder if I would have
grown up liking myself, or whether I
would have had the opportunities I've had.
It's then that I realize again how lucky
I am to have a mother who cares
for me the way you do.
And I feel that I was meant to be
your child, because if I had ever
been given the chance to choose
which mother I would have . . .
I would have chosen you.

—Judith L. Sloan

For All the Times, Mother

For all the times I turn to you
and you are always there,
    I thank you dearly.

For all the times when you are
my sun smiling through in
a cloudy sky,
    I thank you warmly.

For all the times you tell me
that tomorrow will be better,
    I thank you for helping me
    to make it so.

For all the times I count on you,
I thank you with all my heart
for never letting me down.

For all you do, and
for all you have done,
I thank you with everything within me.
And I want you to know,
even if I don't always say so,
    that appreciating you
        is something I have always done
        and something I will
                always do.

— Collin McCarty

I Feel So Proud
to Be Your Child

You are a remarkable woman
who accomplishes so much as a
strong woman
in a man's world
You are strong but soft
You are strong but caring
You are strong but compassionate

You are a remarkable woman
who accomplishes so much as a
giving woman
in a selfish world
You give to your friends
You give to your family
You give to everyone

You are a remarkable woman
who is also a remarkable mother
And you are loved by so many people
whose lives you have touched —
especially me

—Susan Polis Schutz

My Feelings for My Mother

Whenever I get lonely,
all I have to do is
imagine myself home with you.

You're the person
who means the most to me
in my life,
and it sometimes makes me
sad to think that we don't
see each other more often
than we do.

But though we're not together
as often as I'd like us to be,
we are — and always will be —
together in so many
wonderful family feelings.
The most special place
in my heart
will always be saved
for you.

— Collin McCarty

Mother . . . A Family Is Love

Wherever we go,
and whatever we do,
let us live with this
remembrance in our hearts . . .
that we are family.

What we give to one another
comes full circle.
May we always be
the best of friends;

may we always be one another's
   rainbow on a cloudy day;
as we have been yesterday
and today to each other,
      may we be so blessed
         in all our tomorrows . . .
            over and over again.

For we are a family,
   and that means love
         that has no end.

                    — Collin McCarty

There are moments
every day
when I think of you, Mother

You could have just told me how to be
and what to become, but instead,
you showed me how to question and choose
my own destiny.
You could have left me alone when I was
learning to walk,
but you held my hands and shared in my joy,
because it was your joy as well.
You read me stories and enjoyed
my make-believe world,
watching my creativity grow instead of
closing that part of my mind.
You presented me with choices when
I was wrong,
and you gave me wisdom
when I was mistaken.

You always let me try things my way,
and in the times when I failed,
you helped me to pick up the pieces and
    put them together another way.
You taught me how to
    turn failure into success.
You listened to all of my stories,
and your patience taught me how to listen
    to others and really hear them.
You are a part of my every happiness and
    every tear.
Every day you share more love
    and more of yourself
    than I ever thought possible.
When I think of all you put into being
    my mother,
my emotions overcome me.
There are no words to describe
    how much I will always love you
for all that you are, my dearest mother.

—Katie Bindschadler

Mother, the World Needs More
People like You

People like you
are few and far between.
You are the special
   kind of person
      the world needs more of . . .

People like you
make everything so much nicer;
you have a marvelous ability
to turn happiness into joy
and sadness into understanding.

You are loved . . .
         for so many reasons,
and appreciated beyond words,
because people like you
   mean the world to . . .
         people like me.

— Collin McCarty

Our Relationship Is One of
the Best Parts of My Life

You have always
been there for me:
to cry with me
when my heart was broken,
to celebrate my accomplishments,
and to share with me
the wisdom you gained
throughout the years.
When I think back
on my life,
I wonder if I would
have ever made it
without you.

Even now, I rely on
your love and encouragement
to get me through the rough times.
And I anxiously share with you
the joys and excitement
that come my way.
I know I may not
tell you often,
but I hope you'll always
realize how very much
I love you.

—Chris Ardis

To My Mother

When you have a mother
who cares so much for you
that anything you want
comes before her desires
When you have a mother
who is so understanding that
no matter what is bothering you
she can make you smile
When you have a mother
who is so strong that
no matter what obstacles she faces
she is always confident in front of you
When you have a mother
who actively pursues her goals in life
but includes you in all her goals
you are very lucky indeed
Having a mother like this
makes it easy to grow up
into a loving, strong adult
Thank you for
being this kind
of wonderful
mother

— Susan Polis Schutz

Mother,

it takes a long time
for a person to grow, to mature,
and to really understand
what life is all about.
Perhaps that is why
it is only now that I have begun
to really conceive of
how much you have given me,
how hard you have worked,
how often you have laughed,
strived, cried, ached,
rejoiced, and smiled —
all for me!

I know I may not have shown it
as often as I should have,
but the things you have done
have meant more to me than
anything ever has.
I wonder if the words . . .

"Thank you"
and
"I love you"

could possibly say
all that I feel
for you?

—Kristine Jackson

Mother, you're held close in my heart

There are few doors in my life that
I can enter without first knocking —
carrying no gift, no invitation, just
myself — and feel the immediacy of a
genuine welcome. Home has always been
one.

There are few people in my life who
have seen me at my very worst and my
very best — who I can be with or away
from, yet have no fear of being hastily
judged or unfairly criticized. You
have always been one.

There are few times in my life when
I have told you what you mean to me,
though I often believe you already
know. But I want this to be one of
those times . . .

For all the comforts of home,
the generous constancy of your love,
you are held warmly in my
thoughts, close in my heart,
and always with love and affection.

— Carol Ann Oberg

Mother, I Will Always Love You
Much More than You Will Ever Know

In my solitary moments, Mother,
I often take the time to reflect on you,
and I realize that being a mother
is a lifelong commitment to selflessness.
I think that motherhood must be
the most difficult commitment to pursue,
as more often than not,
it requires much more giving than receiving.
The rewards of this commitment
seem to be so very few,
and the demands so very great.

Few children, and I am one of them, ever take
the opportunity to view the realities of motherhood.
Oftentimes, I am so caught up in my own life that
I fail to realize that I am never alone in any emotion.
For each moment of joy I experience,
there is a silent joy shared by you, my mother,
along with a silent prayer of thanks to God
for the blessing He has given me, your child.
Behind each tear shed and each hurt felt,
there is a silent tear and a silent hurt
felt deep inside your heart.
It's strange that these silent emotions
are never readily apparent,
but they are always behind your words
of encouragement, wisdom, understanding, and faith
that there will be a better tomorrow awaiting me.
I also have silent emotions;
mine are the prayers of thanks to God
that I hold deep within my heart
whenever I reflect upon you, my mother.
I will always love you much more
than you will ever know.

—Catherine I. DiGiorgio

Thank you, Mother . . .

For all the times
I should have said it,
but didn't . . .
Thanks!
For all the times
you deserved to hear it,
but didn't . . .
I appreciate you so much!
And for all the emotion
I feel, but don't always
show it . . .
I love you!

— Bonnie Bachman Bragg

For all that you are, Mother

Mother, you give me love.
You give me gentle encouragement
and tender affection.
I cherish our times together
because you are a sincere friend —
someone I can openly laugh with,
someone I can share a secret with,
someone I can trust and admire.
Our stormy times become fewer
as I grow to realize that our
disagreements are not as important
as the things we stand together on,
and there is never an argument
so important between us to make me
hold back my love from you.

I appreciate and love you, Mother,
for all that you are
and for all that you do.

— Donna Levine